THE CLIMATE CRISIS
– GREENHOUSE EFFECT AND OZONE LAYER

Designed and produced by
Aladdin Books Ltd
70 Old Compton Street
London W1

*First published in the
United States in 1989 by*
Gloucester Press
387 Park Avenue South
New York, NY 10016

Printed in Belgium

Design: Rob Hillier, Andy Wilkinson
Editor: Margaret Fagan

Researcher: Cecilia Weston-Baker
Illustrator: Ron Hayward Associates

Library of Congress Cataloging-in-Publication Data

Becklake, John.
     The climate crisis / by John Becklake.
        p. cm. – (Issues)
     Includes index.
     Summary: Discusses the damage to the ozone layer created
by the dispersal of chemicals into the atmosphere and how
pollutants may be causing the earth's climate to change due to
the greenhouse effect.
     ISBN 0-531-17173-6
     1. Ozone layer--Environmental aspects--Juvenile literature. 2.
Greenhouse effect. Atomspheric--Juvenile literature. (1. Ozone
layer. 2. Greenhouse affect. Atmospheric.) I. Title.
TD885.5.085B4   1989
363.73'92--dc20
                                        89-31780
                                             CIP
                                             AC

Contents

THE CLIMATE CRISIS
—GREENHOUSE EFFECT AND OZONE LAYER

JOHN BECKLAKE

Illustrated by
Ron Hayward Associates

Franklin Watts
New York : London : Toronto : Sydney

Introduction

Suddenly television and newspapers have made us all aware that the climate of the whole Earth may be changing. The greenhouse effect which warms the Earth seems to be increasing as we pour carbon dioxide gas from power stations and cars into the atmosphere. A hole has also appeared in the ozone layer that protects us from dangerous radiation from the Sun. For the first time in history people are causing permanent and alarming changes to the atmosphere. In the past there were local changes due to building towns, draining marshes and cutting down forests. Today, however, a huge world population relies on advanced industries and this has brought large-scale changes and worldwide problems.

Most industry depends on electricity which is generated by burning fossil fuels (coal, oil or gas). Burning fossil fuels produces carbon dioxide and this is gradually building up in the atmosphere. Scientists believe this build-up can disastrously change the climate of the world.

The atmosphere is further threatened by man-made gases which attack the ozone layer. Is it too late to stop or reverse these changes in our atmosphere? Can we persuade all the countries in the world that we must work together to keep our environment safe for us to live in? Or will unchecked pollution of our atmosphere cause a climate crisis? These are the issues which are discussed in this book.

◁ In 1988 farmers in the United States suffered from drought – land that normally grew crops was like dust. If the greenhouse effect makes the Earth hotter, the whole world will see changes in climate like this affecting the environment.

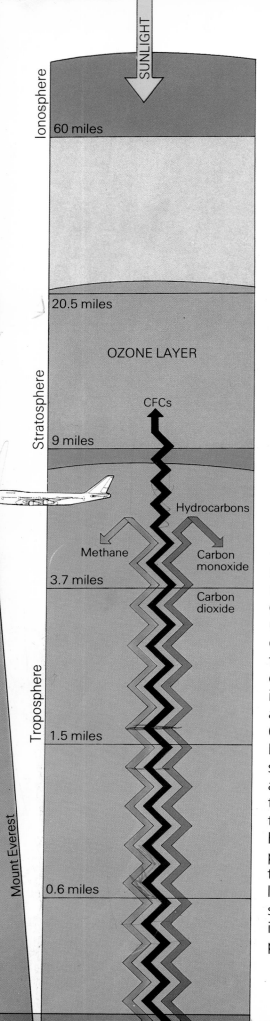

Ionosphere

60 miles

SUNLIGHT

20.5 miles

OZONE LAYER

Stratosphere

CFCs

9 miles

Hydrocarbons

Methane

Carbon
monoxide

3.7 miles

Carbon
dioxide

Troposphere

1.5 miles

0.6 miles

Mount Everest

Changing atmosphere

The layer of gases around the Earth, called the atmosphere, is essential to life on Earth. It supplies oxygen to breathe and protection from harmful radiation from the Sun and from small rocks flying through space. Its movements cause the changing weather which happens in the lower part of the atmosphere as the Sun heats the Earth. The air circulates because the equator is warmer than the poles, so hot air rises near the equator letting cold air rush in from the poles. This is complicated by the spin of the Earth and the position and height of the land and sea below the moving air. It is vey difficult to forecast the weather even with modern computers, but it is even more difficult to predict the climate which is the pattern of weather averaged over a long time.

◁ The atmosphere is a mixture of gases, mainly nitrogen and oxygen, gradually thinning out higher up from the Earth. Carbon dioxide is only a tiny fraction of the atmosphere and ozone even less, but they are very important. Most of the gases are in the lowest layer below 6 miles, the troposphere. Between 6 and 30 miles is the stratosphere. Here ozone absorbs ultraviolet light from the Sun, making the temperature increase with height. Most atmospheric pollution stays in the troposphere but some gases last long enough to reach the stratosphere where the ozone is. High aircraft fly in the lower part of the stratosphere.

▽ All over the world factory chimneys, like these in China, pour out smoke polluting the atmosphere.

All the past changes in the climate have had natural causes but now we are polluting our atmosphere so much that it could change the climate of the whole world. Some polluting gases are man-made gases which last a long time and others come from power stations, factories, cars and intensive farming. They are all building up in the atmosphere, changing its natural balance.

Like the weather, the climate of the Earth is always changing naturally. Over long periods of time, the way the Earth circles the Sun or the tilt of its spin axis changes. In the past the Earth has been both hotter and colder than now. In the last Ice Age, 20,000 years ago, the average temperatures were about 18° F lower than today and ice covered most of Canada, Scandinavia and Russia. We are now in a warmer period, but even within this period there have been variations in climate. In Europe, the 12th and 13th centuries were warmer with vineyards flourishing in Britain and Belgium, while in the 17th century it was colder and Britain's River Thames regularly froze in winter. Then the average world temperature was less than 2° F lower than now. We do not really know what causes these small climate variations, but any temperature change can affect the way we live.

The greenhouse effect

The atmosphere surrounding the Earth acts rather like a greenhouse, keeping the Earth warm and comfortable for life. If the balance of greenhouse gases is disturbed, the planet could become too hot, or too cold, for life.

On a clear day, most of the light from the Sun comes straight through the atmosphere, like sunlight entering a greenhouse through the glass. It warms the land or sea and this then gives out heat. But the heat cannot all escape freely either through the glass in the greenhouse or through the atmosphere. Part of it does escape but the rest is absorbed by some of the gases in the atmosphere which themselves give out heat keeping the air and ground warm. The main gases in the atmosphere, oxygen and nitrogen, take no part in this but they do play their role in spreading the heat evenly around the Earth.

The greenhouse gases
The gases that absorb heat and warm the Earth are only a tiny fraction of the total atmosphere. The major greenhouse gases are carbon dioxide (the gas that makes the bubbles in soft drinks) and water vapor, methane from natural gas, swamps, rice fields, and animals, and nitrous oxide from artificial fertilizers. The CFC gases from spray cans and refrigerators, which destroy the ozone layer, are also very efficient greenhouse gases.

▽ Rice paddy fields contribute to the greenhouse effect.

The problem with the greenhouse effect is that it seems to be increasing. The greenhouse gases are increasing in quantity in the atmosphere mainly due to the actions of human beings. As the population of the world grows ever larger, we release more of the greenhouse gases into the atmosphere by burning more fuels to supply energy, and farming more intensively to provide food. We have even produced man-made gases to run refrigerators and operate spray cans. These gases are better at absorbing heat than the natural gases, and are also building up in the atmosphere. The result of all this is that the Earth is gradually getting hotter. Nobody knows what the consequences will be, but it will probably lead to drastic changes in the climate with more frequent drought in some parts of the world and wetter weather in other places.

▽ Most of the Sun's energy arrives at the Earth as light. The atmosphere and clouds reflect some light back to space, but most reaches the surface, where some more is reflected away by the oceans, ice caps and land. The rest warms the surface which gives out heat. Most of this is absorbed by greenhouse gases in the lower atmosphere, warming the air too. Without the greenhouse effect and the atmosphere, the average temperature over the whole Earth would be about 54° F lower than it is now.

Light reflected back to space

The atmosphere and clouds

Light warms the surface

Light reflected by the oceans

9

△ Nearly all cars burn gasoline or diesel pouring exhaust fumes into the atmosphere. These contain the greenhouse gases carbon dioxide and nitrous oxide as well as the gases which cause smog and acid rain. The electric power used to make these vehicles came from burning coal or oil.

Invisible balance

Carbon dioxide

Build-up of carbon dioxide in the atmosphere

The graph shows how carbon dioxide has been increasing in the atmosphere for about 150 years. Much of this comes from burning fossil fuels. We are also destroying forests which use up carbon dioxide as they grow. At this rate the atmosphere will contain twice as much carbon dioxide by the year 2080 as there was in 1850.

▽ Natural gas contains the greenhouse gas methane. This escapes into the atmosphere from oil wells and pipelines. Even if it is burnt off as in this photograph, it still produces carbon dioxide.

In the past the climate of the Earth has seen dramatic changes, often caused by natural events like volcanic eruptions. But despite the changes the atmospheric gases have stayed in a natural balance, with animals breathing in oxygen and breathing out carbon dioxide, while plants take in carbon dioxide and release oxygen as they grow.

In the last 150 years that balance has been disturbed: man is polluting the atmosphere with gases which increase the greenhouse effect. The increase in the amount of carbon dioxide, the main greenhouse gas, is a major factor but we are adding other gases like methane, the chlorofluorocarbons (CFCs) and nitrous oxide which also damage the balance. Some of these are more efficient greenhouse gases than carbon dioxide. Methane, the natural gas trapped in oil fields, also comes from wet paddy fields, rotting garbage and is released as animals pass wind. CFCs are used in refrigerators, spray cans, polyurethane foam and industrial cleaning processes. They are ten thousand times more effective as greenhouse gases than carbon dioxide. If we keep adding all these gases to the atmosphere at the present rate, scientists expect the average temperature of the Earth to rise by between 3 and 7° F by the year 2030.

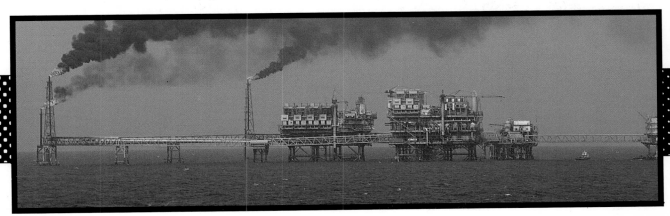

Ruin of the forests

The destruction of major forests all around the world has also contributed to the growing amount of carbon dioxide in the atmosphere. The destruction increases carbon dioxide in two ways. All green plants use up carbon dioxide as they grow, so when forests are destroyed there is less vegetation to remove the carbon dioxide. In addition, burning the forest trees produces carbon dioxide just like burning coal or oil. On the other hand forests absorb more of the Sun's energy than pasture or deserts, so fewer forests would tend to cool the Earth. The overall effects of deforestation are still unknown.

◁ The smoke from burning forests pollutes the atmosphere, adding to the greenhouse effect.

▽ The forest has been destroyed but the land provides crops or grazing for only a few years.

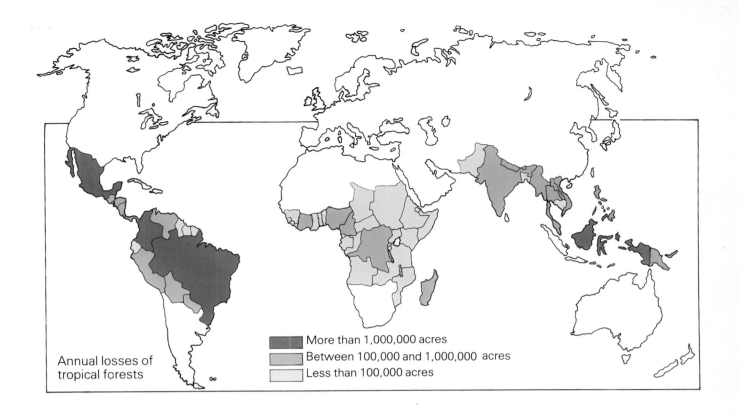

Annual losses of
tropical forests

More than 1,000,000 acres
Between 100,000 and 1,000,000 acres
Less than 100,000 acres

△ Rain forests are being destroyed in tropical countries all around the world. The greatest loss is in Central and South American countries, but India and many African and Southeast Asian countries are also culprits. The land is cleared to grow food and provide exports to earn money. When forests are destroyed the climate gets drier.

Some scientists have suggested planting trees to compensate for the lost forests, but an area the size of France would have to be planted every year to remove all the extra carbon dioxide which is put into the atmosphere. Meanwhile the deforestation continues under pressure from a huge industry of cattle ranching. Stretches of tropical rain forest about the size of Iceland are cleared and burnt every year to provide pasture land to raise cattle for beef – mainly for export. Farmers need grazing land the size of a tennis court to produce just 40 hamburgers per year.

But cleared forest does not make good grazing land for long: it soon becomes exhausted semi-desert, and then more forest must be burnt to feed the cattle. The increasing numbers of cattle also produce more methane, which adds to the greenhouse effect.

Stormy weather

The Earth does seem to be getting hotter. The six hottest years on record were all in the 1980s, and the average world temperature has risen by 1° F (0.5° C) since the beginning of the twentieth century. But that is only the average temperature. Scientists use computers to predict how the climate will change if the Earth gets warmer. Not everywhere will heat up; some places will get cooler, though the changes will affect us all. During the last 20 years Great Britain and Europe have had slightly lower temperatures, and Alaska had its coldest winter in 1988. The unusual weather that many parts of the world have seen in the past few years may already be the first sign of global climate change.

In the Pacific Ocean the trade winds blow from east to west and push the surface water towards the west. The water which wells up to take its place off the coast of South America brings nutrients for the plankton, fish and birds to feed on. Every few years the trade winds weaken. This is called El Nino and the change in the ocean currents can alter the rainfall and temperatures around the world.

△ In 1987, a severe hurricane hit Northern France and Southern England. It was not forecast and did enormous damage. Hurricanes are almost unknown in this area. Storms like this will be more severe and occur more often in a hotter world.

In the 1980s there were severe droughts and famine in East Africa, and flooding in India and Bangladesh. The normally fertile grain belt of the United States suffered a devastating drought in 1988. Something strange seems to be happening to the weather, but is it caused by the greenhouse effect or is it just that the weather has always been extremely variable? Scientists do not really know, and if we continue to put carbon dioxide, CFCs and other greenhouse gases into the atmosphere, we shall only find out after the damage is done. Meanwhile climatologists have linked the recent droughts and the floods in Bangladesh to El Nino. Will the greenhouse effect make El Nino and its consequences even more unpredictable?

▽ Climate changes may make some parts of the world uninhabitable. Machinery is more difficult to operate in the cold, and crops will not grow if it is too hot and dry.

A hotter Earth

Scientists think that the greenhouse effect will make the average temperature of the Earth rise 3-7° F by the year 2030. However they cannot tell in detail what effect this will have on the world's climate. Computer predictions give rough indications of the changes in different areas. The higher temperatures will not be evenly spread: the rise will be higher at the poles than at the equator and the crop growing areas will move away from the equator toward the poles. The major grain belt in the United States will move towards Canada and farmers will have to adapt to these changes. Actually carbon dioxide encourages plant growth, so crop yields may be higher in fertile parts.

Overall the weather will be cloudier and wetter, which could have a cooling effect as the clouds reflect more sunlight back into space. In particular the coastal regions will be wetter. Inland areas will not have much more rain and the higher temperatures will tend to dry out the continent interiors, increasing the desert areas.

Areas wetter than now
Areas drier than now
♦ Major grain areas

On this map you can see the areas that will be wetter or drier than now if the predictions are correct. It also shows where we now grow most of the grain. The grain belts of the United States and the Soviet Union could be drier, growing less wheat, while the semi-desert countries of the Middle East may be able to grow more, changing the balance of world politics.

◁ Small villages like this one on the banks of the Nile would not survive in a hotter world. Their land would become useless and the villagers would have to find a more fertile area. Such resettlements would cause chaos: 50 million people live on the Nile's banks.

△ The 1988 floods in Bangladesh were caused by torrential rains which may have been linked to the greenhouse effect. In a warmer world flooding will become even worse as the sea levels rise, causing loss of life and huge displacements of people.

As the Earth warms up, the water in the oceans expands, raising the sea levels. They have risen by about 6 inches since 1880 and are likely to rise another 12 inches before 2030, flooding low-lying areas. However, if the temperature rises by about 9° F the Antarctic ice cap will start to melt, and raise the sea level by 16 feet or more.

▽ The Great Plains of the United States are one of the world's major grain growing areas, but possibly not for long. They could become hotter, drier, and unsuitable for grains — in fact virtually a desert.

Ozone. . . . .

The ozone layer high up in the atmosphere also influences conditions on Earth. It is not a solid layer, just a region where ozone molecules are constantly being formed and then broken down naturally by sunlight. This process absorbs dangerous ultraviolet radiation and warms the atmosphere. Ozone is made all over the world during the hours of daylight and is carried from place to place by the air currents. The height and thickness of the ozone layer vary in different places and with the time and seasons. The ozone layer is very fragile and we are now discovering how easy it is for pollutants to gobble up the ozone, leaving us without protection from ultraviolet radiation.

◁ The ozone layer above 9 miles high in the atmosphere absorbs the ultraviolet radiation from the Sun. However, in the Antarctic spring most of the ozone above the Antarctic disappears, leaving a hole that lets much more radiation reach the ground.

Ultraviolet radiation

Ozone layer

More ultraviolet radiation reaches Earth

Antarctica

Nimbus measures ozone in the atmosphere, but computers ignored the ozone hole at first.

Ozone

The bluish gas, ozone, is made of oxygen atoms like the oxygen we breathe. Unlike oxygen, ozone consists of three atoms, is poisonous to breathe in and there is hardly any in the lower part of the atmosphere. The fragile ozone layer, high up in the atmosphere, also contains only a very small amount of ozone.

Scientists had measured the amounts of ozone in the layer for many years, fearing it might be damaged by man-made air pollution. Then suddenly in 1985 British scientists announced that they had discovered a 30 percent decrease in the amount of ozone over Halley Bay in the Antarctic. At first they could not believe their measurements — they had expected damage to occur slowly. Also satellite instruments had not detected anything unusual. Then they discovered that the satellite scientists had told their computers to regard any very low readings as errors, and had "missed" the hole. The damage was so dramatic that scientists were extremely concerned.

▽ Balloons carry instruments high into the stratosphere to measure ozone and other gases.

Is the hole dangerous?

▽ In October 1987 the Nimbus 7 satellite measured the amounts of ozone over the Antarctic. The colors in this computer-generated photograph show the levels of ozone, and the hole is the black area in the middle. You can see the white outline of Antarctica underneath the hole. The other outlines, near the edge of the map, are South America, South Africa, Australia and New Zealand, showing how close they are to the hole.

As ultraviolet radiation from the Sun is harmful to most life on Earth, we need protection from it. Ultraviolet is the part of sunlight that causes a suntan – or sunburn. But it also causes skin cancer and eye cataracts. These are the problems that will increase if the ozone layer is damaged.

Animals will have similar problems, and plants will probably not grow as well, so crops will yield less food for animals and humans to eat. These effects will become gradually more severe if the ozone layer gets thinner, but if there was a catastrophic destruction of the ozone layer, life as we know it could not exist on Earth. The only living things would be down in the oceans where the ultraviolet radiation could not reach.

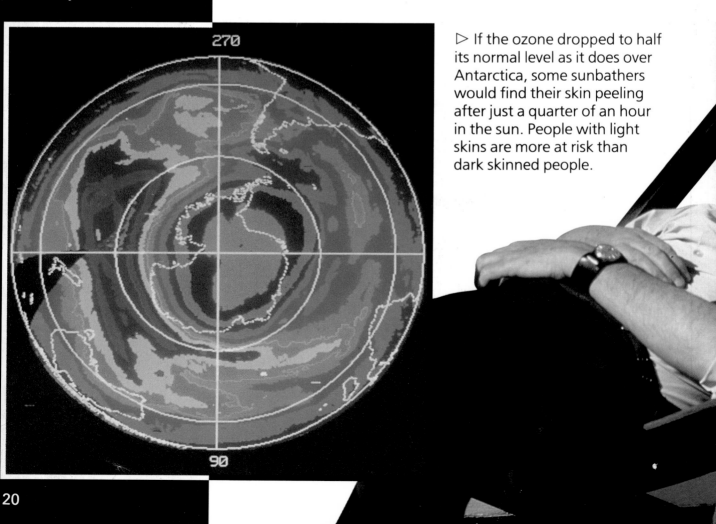

270

90

▷ If the ozone dropped to half its normal level as it does over Antarctica, some sunbathers would find their skin peeling after just a quarter of an hour in the sun. People with light skins are more at risk than dark skinned people.

Consequently the discovery of a hole in the ozone layer over the Antarctic frightened scientists and politicians. Records now show that the hole has appeared every spring since the late 1970s. In 1987 ozone levels dropped by over 50 percent and the hole covered the entire Antarctic continent. It only appears for a short time in spring, then disappears for the rest of the year.

One of the biggest worries was why the hole had appeared so suddenly. Luckily it seems to happen because of the extreme conditions over the South Pole that do not occur anywhere else in the atmosphere. However the concentration of ozone has also decreased by a few percent over populated areas of the northern hemisphere.

▽ Surfers enjoying the sea in South Australia in December 1987 might have been the first people to experience the effects of the ozone hole. That . month the ozone hole was breaking up over Antarctica and some of the upper atmosphere drifted north to Australia, taking part of the hole over populated areas. The ozone levels dropped by 10 percent over Perth, Melbourne, and South Island, New Zealand.

The culprits

The main culprits destroying the ozone layer are the man-made CFC gases, which are doubly dangerous because they are also greenhouse gases. They are used to push the contents out of spray cans, to clean electronic circuits and they are the working liquid sealed inside refrigerators. They are cheap to make and were considered very safe because they do not easily break down into other substances. However this stability has caused the problem. It means that CFCs can drift unchanged up through the atmosphere into the stratosphere.

▽ In many of their uses CFCs can be replaced by less damaging gases, but other culprit gases may not be so easy to replace. Anesthetic gases used in hospitals, like nitrous oxide (laughing gas), are ozone eaters if they can travel up through the atmosphere to the ozone layer in the stratosphere.

▽ CFCs were used in most spray cans until the dangers were realized. Now in many countries this use has been banned and other gases are used instead.

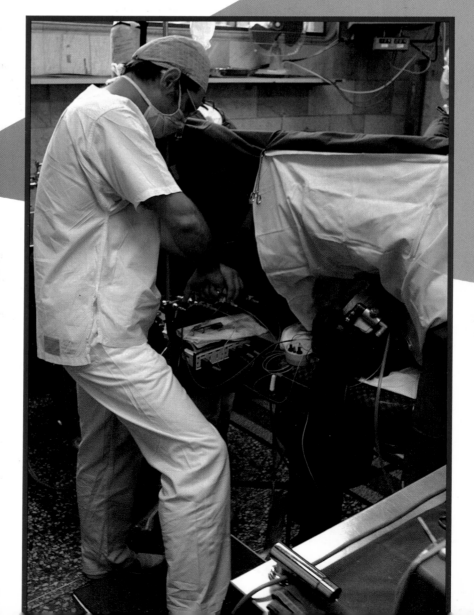

Scientists measuring CFCs in the atmosphere and monitoring the ozone hole, found that as the level of CFCs increased, the amount of ozone decreased. They discovered that in winter when the Sun does not rise, icy clouds form in the stratosphere where the CFCs are. Then when the Sun reappears in spring all the chlorine atoms are released at once to destroy ozone.

CFCs are not the only culprits. Oxides of nitrogen (gases containing oxygen and nitrogen) from nitrogen fertilizers and aircraft engines also destroy ozone. When supersonic aircraft like Concorde were developed in the early 1960s, there were fears that a large fleet of them flying in the stratosphere could damage the ozone layer with their exhaust gases. At present there are not enough Concordes and they fly too low to be a major problem, but supersonic aircraft of the future could cause another threat to the fragile ozone layer.

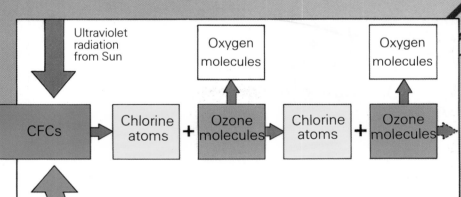

Ultraviolet radiation from Sun

Oxygen molecules

Oxygen molecules

CFCs → Chlorine atoms + Ozone molecules → Chlorine atoms + Ozone molecules →

From spray can

△ Ultraviolet radiation from the Sun splits a chlorine atom from a CFC molecule. This attacks ozone making oxygen molecules, but leaving the chlorine atom free to attack ozone again.

▷ The Space Shuttle's booster rockets deliver ozone destroying gases directly to the stratosphere. In the future, more Space Shuttle flights would bring further pollution.

23

The world's population increase

Destroying our world

◁ More and more people in China want to own a refrigerator so China will continue to produce CFCs unless the richer nations help finance the production of alternatives.

Economic problems
Many poorer countries have borrowed money from richer nations to build schools and hospitals. To repay these loans they produce exports such as beef. But often the rain forest is destroyed to make way for grazing land.

▽ The world's population has increased five times since 1850 and will double again by 2050. All these extra human beings will cause even more pollution, if we can feed them all.

The increasing greenhouse effect and the damage to the ozone layer are causing worldwide problems. These can only be reduced if all the nations work together. Even then there are no easy solutions, especially to the increasing greenhouse effect. At the root of the problem is the growing world population and the divide between the rich and poor nations. The high standard of living in the rich countries depends on industry and a ready supply of energy, both of which contribute to pollution of the environment. Naturally, the poorer nations want to enjoy the same standard of living but this could lead to an increase in pollution. One solution is for the richer nations to reduce their energy demand.

At the same time we must develop alternative energy sources which do not pollute the atmosphere, and clean up our industries to reduce their pollution. But all this will be in vain unless contraception is properly used to control the enormous growth of the world population. This is vital in the poorer countries which have fewer resources to care for their populations and their environment.

6 billion 1996

5 billion 1990

4 billion 1975

2 billion 1930

Caring for our world

Now we are aware of these problems, it may not be too late to preserve our environment for future generations. We know that CFC gases are the main culprits destroying ozone, and industrial chemists are now looking for other gases that could be used in refrigerators. The use of CFCs in spray cans is already being reduced in many countries. The production of greenhouse gases will not be so easy to limit. We need food and energy for the increasing population of the world, and in producing these we increase the greenhouse gases in the atmosphere. We will have to find other sources of energy which do not rely on burning fossil fuels. These include solar and wind power, and energy from the waves and tides. Nuclear power would provide more energy but it brings the dangers of radiation pollution.

So we will all have to be more careful to use less energy and not waste as much as we do now. Also if we eat less meat, there will be fewer animals to produce methane, and less rain forest will be destroyed for grazing land. When looking for solutions to our problems we must be careful that they do not also have other hidden problems for future generations to solve.

Alternatives to CFCs
Alternative gases are already being used in many spray cans and in the manufacture of some insulating boxes and cups. Now chemical companies are looking for other gases to use in refrigerators, but these will be more expensive. Meanwhile we could recycle CFCs, especially those used to clean electronic circuits, and remove them from old refrigerators.

▽ The Sun's energy can be turned into electricity by reflecting it onto a boiler which runs a steam generator. Electricity can also be made directly by using solar cells. This can be done even in cloudy weather. But both methods need a large area to collect much energy.

◁ Nuclear power protesters at Broksdorf, West Germany, are concerned about the safety of nuclear power stations. However these power stations do not burn fossil fuels so they do not produce carbon dioxide to add to the greenhouse effect. Their problems are the dangers of radiation leaks, and disposing of nuclear waste. At present we do not know which problem is worse, but in future we may have to produce more electricity at nuclear power stations.

The future

Unless we can limit the greenhouse gases and ozone-destroying chemicals we pour into the atmosphere, we will live in a much less hospitable world. Changes in climate could cause political instability and the resettlement of millions of people as floods or drought could ruin their livelihood.

However, the changing climate is not the the only problem: pollutants from our homes and factories are poisoning rivers and seas and killing trees. Pollution does not recognize boundaries between countries or peoples, and so its problems can only be solved if all the nations of the world work together. Fortunately scientists have managed to alert the politicians to the dangers and there have been international conferences to discuss the problems of the ozone layer and the greenhouse effect. At a conference in Montreal in 1987, agreements were signed to limit the production of CFCs.

▷ This is the new "ozone-friendly" symbol. It appears on products such as spray cans and shows that there are no damaging CFC gases in the product. If we all insist on buying ozone-friendly products, the manufacturers will soon stop using CFCs altogether.

▽ Planting trees to replace the rain forests will help to reduce the amount of carbon dioxide in the atmosphere. However, trees cannot remove all the extra carbon dioxide from industry.

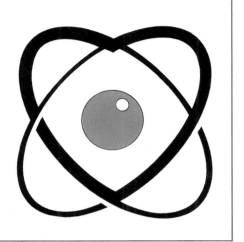

We need to do much more if we are to keep the world safe. In the next 50 years the use of CFCs will have to be phased out. Our fossil-fueled power stations will have to be replaced by other sources of power like nuclear power or solar power, and we will have to use personal transportation less. Fusion power may be a cheap, inexhaustible and safe energy source, if it can be developed on a large scale and has no hidden snags.

If we continue to ignore our impact on the environment, we will not be able to avoid a climate crisis.

▷ At Montreal it was agreed to reduce the release of CFCs by 50 percent by the end of the century. But general industrial pollution also needs to be limited.

Hard Facts

The burning of fossil fuels and the use of CFCs have been the main causes of change to the greenhouse effect and the ozone layer.

Carbon Dioxide Emissions from Fossil Fuels

The industrial nations are the main producers of carbon dioxide. The United States, Soviet Union and Europe together are responsible for over 60% of the world output of carbon dioxide. The developing countries only contribute about 15% now but this will increase. The table below illustrates how much carbon dioxide each country produces.

United States	22%
Soviet Union	18%
Western Europe	14%
China	11%
Eastern Europe	7%
South America	4%
India	3%
Africa	3%
Middle East	3%

Carbon Dioxide in the Atmosphere

The amount of carbon dioxide in the atmosphere has been measured regularly for the past 25 years at the Mauna Loa Observatory in Hawaii. This shows a steady increase from 315 parts per million in 1957 to nearly 350 parts per million now. Other measurements show that this increase started from a natural level of about 270 parts per million around 1850. At the present rate of increase the amount of carbon dioxide will be double its original natural level by about 2080.

Chlorofluorocarbons (CFCs)

These are very stable man-made chemicals containing chlorine, fluorine and carbon. There are many different CFCs but the ones that destroy the most ozone in the stratosphere are CFC11 and CFC12. The one used to clean electronic circuits is CFC113. In 1986 about 30% of CFCs were used in spray cans, nearly 34% in the production of foam insulating materials, and another 30% in air conditioning units and refrigerators. The annual consumption of CFCs in the United States is 0.9 kg (2lb) per person, in Western Europe 0.8 kg (1.5lb) per person, but worldwide, only 0.2 kg (0.4lb) per person. Some CFCs are so stable they can persist in the atmosphere for over 100 years. Even if the release of all CFCs into the atmosphere was stopped the ozone destruction would continue to increase for about another 20 years, and 40% of the CFCs would still be there at the end of the 21st century.

Environmental Organizations

There are two main international environmental organizations you can join if you want to help. They are concerned with air and water pollution, agricultural chemicals and nuclear power issues. Friends of the Earth campaign for the preservation of the rain forests. Greenpeace actively pursues the idea of an unexploited Antarctic Continent.

Friends of the Earth
530 7 Street SE,
Washington, D.C. 20003

Greenpeace International
1436 U Street NW,
Washington, D.C. 20009

1800 The Industrial Revolution is in full swing in Great Britain and spreading across the world. Fossil fuels are now used for industrial power.

1863 British scientists John Tyndall describes how water vapor in the atmosphere helps to keep the world warm.

1896 Svante Arrhenius of Sweden warns that the carbon dioxide entering the atmosphere from burning coal for industrial power is likely to make the world warmer.

1930 Thomas Midgley, an American engineer, suggests using the newly produced CFCs instead of poisonous ammonia in refrigerators.

1957 During the International Geophysical Year, researchers in Antarctica and Hawaii begin regular monitoring of atmospheric carbon dioxide and the ozone layer.

1960s The dangers to the ozone layer from high flying aircraft are investigated.

1970s The potential dangers of CFCs to the ozone layer are realized by environmental groups. In the United States manuacturers are forced to reconsider the use of CFCs in spray cans. This is the first and easiest step.

1975 Verabhadran Ramanathan identifies CFCs as very strong greenhouse gases.

1982 A "hole" in the ozone layer is first detected by the British Antarctic Survey team led by Joe Farman. They were not confident of these results and did not publish them until the hole, now bigger, had been monitored in 1983 and 1984.

1987 The Montreal Convention is held to discuss how to limit atmospheric pollution by CFCs. It was soon followed by other meetings to consider this and the greenhouse effect.

1989 Scientists and politicians are more aware of the urgent need to protect the environment. Public attention is focused on the problems of the greenhouse effect and the ozone layer.

▽ Alternative gases are replacing CFCs in the manufacture of insulating cups and cartons such as those used to keep hamburgers warm. Many companies have responded to the pressure of the environmental lobby and ensure their products are not so harmful to the environment.

Index

Photographic Credits:
Cover and pages 4-5, 6-7, 14, 15, 16-17, 17, 22, 25, 26-27, 27 and back cover: Frank Spooner Agency; pages 8-9, 10, 12-13 and 22: Robert Harding Library; pages 11, 16, 21, 24, 28 and 31: Hutchinson Library; page 18: Neville Kidger / NASA; pages 19, 20 and 28-29: Rex Features; pages 20-21 and 29: Barry Lewis / Network Photographers; page 23: Associated Press.

PRINTED IN BELGIUM BY
proost
INTERNATIONAL BOOK PRODUCTION